STEAM MEMORIES: 1950's

No.15: SHEFFIELD

Including: Sheffield Midland, Victoria, Great Central and Midland Main Lines

INTRODUCTION

This album is composed of illustrations captured by the camera of the late Keith Pirt during the period from the early to the late fifties' in and around the great city of Sheffield. Having the main lines of two former pre Grouping companies, and later two of the Big Four railways within its boundaries, Sheffield could indeed boast to being a great motive power centre.

Keith Pirt travelled all over Sheffield and its outskirts to places which he decided would make ideal locations in which to photograph the rich and diverse collection of locomotives in daily use. Besides the stations and engine sheds, KRP managed to capture some of the industrial 'feel' of the city, warts and all. The pollution, dirt and grime of the period is well depicted between the trains threading their way amongst the natural and man-made obstacles. The leafy suburbs at the southern side of the city are also included to show that Sheffield was not just an industrial powerhouse.

Hopefully, the balance of Eastern and Midland subjects is about right but the album does not claim to portray the history of the railways in and around Sheffield. Instead, it focuses on one decade when the railways themselves were in transition and the old was being discarded for the new.

David Allen, Newstead, October 2008.

(Title page) **Millhouses Standard Class 5 No.73016 gets an early afternoon Sheffield (Midland)—Stockport (Tiviot Dale) stopping train on its way along the Up slow line just south of Midland station in April 1958. The Down fast line can be seen clearly here on the left, in its own cutting, at a lower level than the other running lines. At this point the Down fast line is rising steadily after burrowing beneath the Up and Down slow lines (the two middle tracks) a few hundred yards behind the photographer. The Up and Down fast lines might well have been described as those forming the main line to the south, via Chesterfield, whilst the Up and Down slow lines formed the lines for the Hope Valley route. That, in practice, is how they lined up at Dore & Totley station where they met and ran on the same alignment all the way to Queens Road. However, to get the main line expresses from the eastern side of the railway to the western side, enabling them access to platforms 1 or 2 at Midland station without conflicting movements and the inevitable delays, the 'dive under' became a practical proposition for the MR. The 'dive under' or burrowing junction came about when the Midland decided in 1898 to quadruple the main line from Pond Street, as the MR station was then called, south as far as Dore & Totley. In the twenty-eight years since the opening of the line from Tapton junction where the 'Old road' (North Midland Railway) took a north-easterly course to by-pass Sheffield, the passenger and goods traffic passing through Pond Street station had grown to a position where the station, and its southern approach in particular had become a bottleneck. By 1902 the widening and the 'dive under' was all but complete, however, the enlargement of Pond Street station was not completed until 1905. *BLP 172.1.***

Printed and bound by The Amadeus Press, Cleckheaton, West Yorkshire
First published in the United Kingdom by Book Law Publications, 382 Carlton Hill, Nottingham, NG4 1JA

J11 No.64373 gets the 12.03 p.m. Hull service on its way and is passing Blast Lane goods depot some seventeen minutes late on Sunday 29th June 1958. The 0-6-0 was not originally rostered to work this passenger service but the designated engine, K3 No.61833, was suddenly purloined by control to haul the 11.50 a.m. Marylebone express which required different motive power due to an engine failure. The express itself got away some eighteen minutes late. Keith Pirt noted that No.64373 was in a very poor condition and although normally capable of working such a train as far as Hull, it may not have completed its task. However, Doncaster was the next stop and they probably had something more suitable if not more mechanically sound to take the train onto Hull (Paragon). Note the ever present Victoria station pilot on the left in the shape of one of Darnall's slowly decreasing fleet of C13s. *BLP 185.3.*

Thompson B1 No.61142 of Immingham shed approaches the GC main line overbridge as it works an excursion train along the Midland main heading, via the Hope Valley, for Blackpool and its illuminations on Sunday 12th October 1958. The last few minutes of the trains journey so far have been spent on a viaduct overlooking industrial premises but now, before entering Midland station, the train will spend a little time in a semi-subterranean existence traversing the Nunnery area, which would hardly be noticed by its pleasure seeking passengers. At the rear of the train can be seen Attercliffe Road station which opened with this line in February 1870 and managed to stay in business until the end of January 1995. The middle of the formation is passing over the old Sheffield & South Yorkshire Navigation one of the earlier transport arteries linking Sheffield with the outside world. To the right of the locomotive is a spur leading into one of the Sheffield Corporation Highways depots, this one bounded by two railways, a canal and Bernard Road, access to which was gained at its eastern end. By now the railway spur, which was put in during the late nineteenth century, seems defunct with the Highways and Cleansing departments storing their discarded road vehicles and equipment over the rusting rails. It would be interesting to know why such a connection was required by that particular department of the corporation. On its return from the west coast resort, the B1 made its way to Doncaster where on Tuesday 14th October it entered the Plant works to start a five week long General overhaul. *BLP 204.3.*

Having passed beneath the GC main line, the Midland continues south through a rock cutting (4F No.44426 on an Up freight is demonstrating for us) and passes under the single span stone arch bridge which carried the single track of the Nunnery Colliery railway. Even in this black and white picture, taken during one of Britain's dirtiest decades, in a city not renown for its clean air, one can still spot the coal dust, put down over decades of use, lining the course of the colliery branch. The other black and grey textures are formed from soot. This is October 1958 during an exceptionally bright and clear day. The sunshine enabled Keith Pirt to take this and other views which manage to convey something of the railway infrastructure surrounding this fascinating section of the city. Much has changed here over the last half century, road development has transformed the place but apparently the stone arch of the Nunnery Colliery line remains in situ and will no doubt stay until it is deemed unsafe or is in the way of further redevelopment. *BLP 205.4.*

Looking east along the GC main line we see 'Director' No.62664 PRINCESS MARY slowly approaching Victoria station with a stopping train from Nottingham (Victoria) via Chesterfield (Central) in the summer of 1958. Immediately below us, in the foreground, is the elaborate iron parapet of the bridge spanning the Midland main line. Railway cabins and sheds of varying usage dominate the centre ground whilst beyond them, the line of tall brick buildings marks the Nunnery curve. Behind the camera is Blast Lane goods depot where rail, road and canal met in quiet harmony - at least for a while. *BLP 192.1.*

Looking south now and viewed from the colliery line bridge, C14 No.67447 works a local from Midland station to Barnsley (Court House) on a summer morning in 1958. Eventually to be superseded by diesel multiple units, this service had been plying this route for nearly five years since it was transferred from Victoria station and the GC line to the Midland. The last passenger train from Sheffield (Victoria) to Barnsley (Court House) ran on Saturday 5th December 1953 and was hauled by C13 No.67411. The last train in the opposite direction was hauled by C13 No.67434. Services from Midland station started the following Monday. Even then, before the completion of the electrification of the Woodhead line, the gradual run-down of Victoria was beginning to take shape but it would take a number of years to entirely eliminate the traffic. *BLP 191.8.*

Nunnery junction from the south-west on a sunny morning in October 1958. Judging by the number of trainspotters perched somewhat precariously on the wall bordering Bernard Road, it must have been half-term. Obviously the perch was ideal for spotting anything on the 'Midland' and the branch up to Nunnery sidings, Nunnery curve. The view over the GC, with its sea of catenary, would have been panoramic but somewhat difficult to spot engine numbers unless some enterprising person had a pair of binoculars! It is arguable to state that the signal box (NUNNERY MAIN LINE JUNCTION) and its adjacent junction were forever in shadow, the Sun's rays rarely penetrating the gloom, but occasionally it was bathed in sunshine, albeit briefly during the longer days of June (*see* previous illustration). However, to the 'spotters' of Sheffield it was a good location. Besides this place being one of the city's gloomiest railway installations, it was also one of the most interesting. KRP took this photograph from the bridge which carried the public road over the former London & North Western Railway's City branch into the city centre and into its large goods warehouse. That company came into Sheffield during 1895 from the east by way of the GCR and at Woodbourn (latterly Woodburn) junction the LNWR built its own line which branched off the main line near Nunnery Colliery. Burrowing under the colliery lines and Woodbourn Road, the two track 'Wessy' branch continued west to a patch of ground near Bernard road where it built a goods depot. By 1903 it had tunnelled through the rock escarpment prominent on the right of the picture and built a branch which spanned the Midland before entering its new city centre goods warehouse on Wharf Street. On the Down main a train is 'pegged' adding to the excitement of the morning - what would it be? The arch bridge spanning the main line just by the signal carried the Nunnery Colliery railway into a landsales yard and canal basin adjacent to Blast Lane goods depot. That line too had a torturous route from the colliery to the yard and, just beyond the bridge spanning the curve, it also burrowed through the rock to come out next to the LNW tunnel but at a high enough level to span the LNW branch. Two more tunnels then had to be negotiated in the next half mile before the colliery was reached. *BLP 205.3.*

Returning to our perch over the Midland but turning around virtually 180 degrees to the west, the camera lens finds the eastern throat of Victoria station in July 1958 with K3 No.61944 accelerating away with a service to Hull. In the carriage sidings EM1 Bo-Bo No.26029 is coupled to the stock of Manchester (London Road) bound service which will proceed to Victoria once the K3 and its train and a waiting 'Director' have cleared the road. *BLP 192.2.*

Another Down, all stations morning service from Nottingham (Victoria) via the Chesterfield loop approaches Sheffield with a 'Director' in charge. It is July 1958 and this is No.62663 PRINCE ALBERT from Darnall shed. 1958 was perhaps the 'swansong' year of this class. Having virtually congregated at 41A, the summer of 1958 was the last time when all eleven D11 were active together. Winter storage was followed by summer storage for some in 1959, with No.62665 MONS being condemned in May of that year. The following year brought elimination of the remaining members of the class though happily one was preserved. On the left the view is dominated by Blast Lane goods yard where one of the growing band of 350 h.p. 0-6-0DE shunters is taking care of business. By the end of 1960 some thirty-four of these handy and reliable locomotives were working in the Sheffield District of the Eastern Region, all allocated to Darnall depot, with more yet to arrive from the makers. When the first batch of diesel shunters arrived at Darnall in February 1957 (Nos.13331—13336) footplate staff were sent on training courses at Wath but within weeks the local union (Darnall branch) demanded that the new locomotives be double manned. BR's response was to move the diesels away from Darnall and keep the ancient N5 tank engines on the various shunting duties. Grimesthorpe depot on the Midland had been using the diesel shunters successfully since the previous June but they might as well have been on another planet. Common sense eventually prevailed and the diesels then ousted the 0-6-2Ts into redundancy. *BLP 192.3.*

Later that day a Hull—Liverpool (Central) service approached Victoria with B16/1 No.61412 in charge. These former North Eastern 4-6-0s were regular visitors to Sheffield on these trains. No.61412 was based at Neville Hill and was no doubt being used by Botanic Gardens shed (then in the throes of rebuilding into a diesel depot) as a filling-in turn. The B16 would return to Hull on an evening working after which it would be made ready for working back to Leeds. In December 1960 this engine, along with ten other members of the class, transferred to the former Lancashire & Yorkshire shed at Mirfield of all places but there was little work for them there and by September 1961 they were all condemned and sent to Darlington for scrapping. *BLP 192.6.*

In between the passenger trains using Victoria station, a large number of goods trains traversed the Up and Down goods lines situated on the north side of the platforms. The Up goods workings could perform their west to east journeys without conflicting with other traffic but the Down trains had to cross the Up and Down mains at the west end of the station so that their movements were closely monitored by Control. O4 No.63574 has no such problems as it hauls its mixed freight past Victoria No.4 signal box in August 1958. This Darnall based engine was one of the original Great Central 8K class and was built by North British Locomotive Co. in November 1912. Its LNER classification was O4/1 and this was never altered throughout its lifetime so that when withdrawn in September 1962 it was still in original condition although during the intervening fifty years it had carried fifteen different boilers, albeit all to the same Diagram. These engines were workhorses by any standards and No.63574 had certainly served the LNER well. From its original home at Annesley it went to the former Great Eastern depot at March for a three year stint. Leaving the Fens in April 1932 it moved back to GC country at Mexborough, hauling almost exclusively coal for the next twelve years. Wartime played havoc with locomotive allocations and in September 1944, as LNER No.6227, it went to Colwick, the ex Great Northern shed which was no stranger to the O4 class. Shortly after British Railways came into being the 2-8-0 was given its last transfer and ended up at Darnall. Following withdrawal it was sold to a scrap merchant in the Staffordshire, along with sixteen other members of the class. *BLP 193.4.*

Members of the Gresley D49 'Hunt' or 'Shire' class were once regular visitors to Victoria but by 1958 their visits were down to one a day on a passenger working from Hull. In August 1958 No.62720 CAMBRIDGESHIRE had charge of a return working and is seen departing Victoria in a deplorable state. Based at Botanic Gardens shed since June 1943, except for its first four years in traffic, this 4-4-0 spent the whole of its life working from depots in the East Riding of Yorkshire at either Botanic Gardens, Bridlington or Scarborough. Now approaching its final year of operation, No.62720 would have one more transfer, in June 1959, and that was to Dairycoates shed where most of the Botanic steam locomotives moved when the former twin roundhouse depot became fully dieselised. Spending most of its Dairycoates period in store, the 4-4-0 was condemned in October 1959 and made the one-way journey to Darlington and oblivion. *BLP 193.5.*

13

At the start of 1958 the C13 class was greatly reduced from its original forty members to just ten, most of the withdrawals occurring during the previous six years. In 1958 further inroads were made into the class by withdrawals so that by years end just one would remain in stock. No.67424 was one of a pair (the other was No.67439) allocated to Darnall and used on the Victoria station pilot turns. Both were kept in fairly good condition, for 41A, and both lasted until November 1958 when their condemnation left just No.67417, a long-standing resident of Gorton which managed to keep going until the end of January 1960. However, we are highlighting our local pair in this section of the album and here outside Victoria in September 1958 our first 4-4-2T is seen propelling a Midland Region parcels van towards the station in glorious morning sunshine. Note the condition of the engine which was a credit to both the crew and Darnall's meagre band of cleaners. This engine had spent much of its long life in the Manchester area at either Gorton or Trafford Park with a week spent at Northwich in 1930 and a whole year spent in Wrexham during WWII. It transferred across the Pennines to Darnall (its first foray east of Woodhead) in 14 May 1953. *BLP 196.1.*

The other member of the 'Darnall Two' No.67439 has a break during shunting operations at Bernard Road sidings. Its external condition is not as good as No.24's even though both locomotives last underwent General overhauls in the first half of 1955. As usual the engine crew are greeting Keith Pirt whom by now was well known to most of the 41A footplate staff if not those from other depots who frequented Sheffield on a regular basis. Note the *MASTER CUTLER* Pullman stock (laid up for the weekend) behind the engine is carrying roof boards stating [KING'S CROSS - SHEFFIELD] with no mention of good old Victoria! Like No.24, No.39 also came to Darnall in 1953 from Gorton but a month earlier. It too had spent much of its life working around the Manchester area with a few dabbles at Chester, Wrexham and Northwich. However, it was not the 4-4-2Ts first transfer to Yorkshire because from 20th September 1941 it was resident at Bradford Bowling Jct. shed for three months. They say that 'there is safety in numbers' but not as far as these two engines were concerned. On Friday 14th November 1958 both tanks' were condemned and next morning they were towed, together, over Woodhead and into Gorton works yard where they were broken up. *BLP 195.7.*

Time for some messing about. Or so it might appear. Like a scene from a 19th century event during the building of the great railroads of the United States, our two C13s meet on the same stretch of track virtually buffer to buffer. Of course there was nothing either great or sinister in this meeting just two working 'pilots' going about their tasks in near proximity to each other. Though we took it mostly for granted, it was one of the wonders of the age for enthusiasts travelling by rail through heavily industrialised conurbations seeing, or so it seemed, a different locomotive going about its business every few yards, and on both sides of your train. Of course, new territory brought new excitement but we tended all the same to regard our own local railway scene as boring whereas somebody from fifty miles away of less would have the excitement we ourselves got when we travelled further afield. Summer 1958 was a good time for train spotting -so much was happening, so many changes taking place. People like KRP kept an eye on their local railway scene and photographed most of the new events. When nothing new was taking place they captured daily occurrences like this and thankfully they did. *BLP 196.5.*

Whilst No.67424 gets to grips with a pair of vans and a brake, *THE SOUTH YORKSHIREMAN* gets underway from Victoria at 11.27 a.m. with Stanier Class 5 No.45186 in charge. Motive power for this train, south from Sheffield, was usually provided by Leicester Central shed and the engine would arrive in Victoria with the 7.32 a.m. Leicester—Manchester working. Detaching for either a B1 or, from 1954, electric traction to take the train on to London road, the Leicester engine proceeded to Darnall for servicing in time to get back to Victoria for the Up service to Marylebone from Bradford. During the summer of 1958 some unusual locomotive classes hauled this named train between Sheffield and London. At least three K3s and numerous Stanier Class 5s were observed but in July and August no less than five BR Standard 9F 2-10-0s, from a variety of depots, hauled the Up service. Although the A3s and V2s had once dominated the service, when the London Midland had taken over GC main line in 1958, former ER motive power became rather rare overnight. Above the roofs of the second and third coaches can be seen a pair of EM1 Bo-Bos and a steam locomotive waiting for a path through the station. Like I've already mentioned, locomotives were everywhere. *BLP 196.7.*

Here is something you will not see today - a horsebox special - four four-wheeled vehicles complete with a passenger vehicle for the grooms and attendants. Where this special was going or where it had originated is uncertain but most probably it originated at Aintree and was bound for Newmarket. During the pre-war days of the LNER, D16s would run these trains through from Newmarket to Aintree via Sheffield (Victoria). One thing is for certain, such traffic was lost to road transport. The B1 is No.61316 of Mexborough and the period is late summer 1958. Note the express headlamps. *BLP 200.3*.

Shortly after the passage of the horsebox special, this combination, also sporting express headlamps, approached Victoria from the east. The stock appears to be mainly Gresley in design but the train engine is Thompson B1 No.61124 whilst the pilot engine is Robinson J11 No.64445. The B1 was from Doncaster but the 'Pom-Pom' was one of Darnall's 'dirty' gang. Speculation as to the origins and destination of the train could bring up numerous permutations. As for the presence of the grimy 0-6-0; well possibly it was a rescue engine sent to help an ailing B1? Many of Keith Pirt's original logs have been mislaid so this working shall remain a mystery for the time being at least. Enjoy the sight anyway. *BLP 200.4.*

As mentioned elsewhere the Darnall 'Directors' were finding it harder and harder to secure regular employment during 1958 but even so their external appearance, in the main, was reasonable. No.62662 PRINCE OF WALES still sports its full BR lining on black paint in this September 1958 view of it resting on the Middle road at Victoria. However, the D11 was not waiting for an eastbound working to arrive, instead it was relegated to Victoria station pilot duties. Judging by the amount of coal in the tender it would not get too far anyway - but at least it was still active. Five of the Darnall 'Directors' were put into storage at Staveley shed once the winter timetable was brought in and some of those engines would never work again. Note the lack of overall roof now that electrification has arrived at this station. Also note the original timber clad platform buildings on 4 and 5 platforms. It wasn't all gloom at Victoria because in July a new refreshment room opened on the Down island platform, Nos.2 and 3. It was described as 'very spacious and of the latest contemporary design'. It replaced the original GCR buffet. These were the second such facilities opened to the public that year. *BLP 202.4.*

Sheffield (Victoria)—Nottingham (Victoria); Sheffield (Victoria)—York; Sheffield (Victoria)—Cleethorpes were just some of the trains which employed the 'Directors in their final years at Darnall. The former route could take them main line to Nottingham or via the Chesterfield loop. This is No.62663 PRINCE ALBERT again but now it is October 1958 and the 4-4-0 is once again in charge of a return working from Nottingham. Besides the D11 class, B1 and K3 classes also worked these trains but during the last week of February 1959 a most unusual engine at the head of the 10.8 a.m. service from Sheffield (Victoria) to Nottingham (Victoria) was Stanier 'Crab' No.42983, which was having a short 'unofficial' residence at Annesley. It was rare to see these 2-6-0 tender engines away from the Western Lines of the LM Region but to see one working a GC Line stopping passenger train was an event worth recording. Unfortunately its visit was not recorded on film - at least by KRP. *BLP 200.7.*

One former LNER class common in Sheffield which we have not featured yet is the Gresley J39 so here is Retford based No.64893 seen gingerly traversing the goods lines between Woodburn and Nunnery junctions (note Woodbourn bridge in the distance and the main lines on the right) with a heavy west bound mineral working. This train most probably originated in the Worksop area and the J39 would uncouple here to run back eastwards with empties. These powerful yet versatile 0-6-0s became the LNER Group Standard six-coupled goods engines and no less than 289 were constructed between September 1928 and August 1941. Having vacuum brakes fitted made them instantly useful for mixed traffic work too. Built at Darlington in October 1935, as No.2989, this engine had used no less than five of the main LNER locomotive workshops for overhauls and repairs but during November and December 1950 it was one of 159 members of the class overhauled at the LMR locomotive works at Derby - that workshop apparently liked 0-6-0s no matter what their origin. Its final visit to 'shops' was to Stratford in April 1960 when that works scrapped it during the mass slaughter of the class which lasted from May 1959 to December 1962. Despite one engine (No.64747) escaping the cull until December 1964, having been withdrawn but hiding away on Stationery Boiler duties at Woodford Halse shed, not one member of the class was preserved! *BLP 202.8.*

Woodburn junction was one of the great meeting places for lines east of Victoria station. Created in 1864 when the South Yorkshire Railway gained access to MS&L's Sheffield (Victoria) passenger station - the route, via Attercliffe, became steeper with each yard and before Woodburn junction was reached the gradient was an impressive 1 in 72. Here in October 1958 Doncaster based B1 No.61193 passes the 105 lever signal box with an express. The 4-6-0 is just about to traverse the rails of the junction which could take it left onto the SYR line and then northwards to Rotherham and Doncaster, or straight on along the main line. To the left of the signal box is the former LNWR route to City goods. The first of the electrification catenary posts were erected here in 1953 and by the end of 1954 the job was completed as far as Rotherwood exchange sidings, nearly three miles further to the east. With the opening of the new marshalling yard at Tinsley, the SYR route was electrified in 1965. Just a few hundred yards east of where the photographer is standing, another junction (Darnall West junction) branches off the main line, in a north-westerly direction, to connect with the SYR line at what became known as Attercliffe junction. Opened in 1873, this line enabled trains from the east and south to proceed northwards without having to use Victoria for reversal. Two years later the SYR became part of the MS&LR empire. *BLP 203.2.*

Many of the GC 'Directors' managed to keep their fully lined BR livery towards the end of their lives but class leader No.62660 BUTLER HENDERSON had to make do with unlined black after a visit to Gorton in the summer of 1957. But, it was the engine chosen for the *Railway Correspondence & Travel Society South Yorkshire No.4* rail tour on 21st September 1958. Here at the west end of Darnall shed yard on that morning the D11 is nicely turned out to haul the first section of the tour from Victoria to Wakefield. Although carrying a 41A Darnall shedplate, the 4-4-0 was actually sub-shedded to Staveley to whence it returned after coming off the penultimate leg of the rail tour at Shireoaks. Of course a couple of years in unlined black, with a coat of grime for most of that time, did not do No.62660 any harm as it eventually ended up in Great Central livery as part of the National Collection. *BLP 197.6.*

Staveley Barrow Hill 4F No.43900 pushes empty stock over Bernard Road bridge and into Nunnery carriage sidings on 4th October 1958. Note the NUNNERY SINGLE LINE JUNCTION signal box perched at the top of the gradient encountered by trains using the Nunnery curve. *BLP 199.4.*

Seen from the carriage sidings throat featured in the last illustration, but now looking towards the west, Leicester Central Class 5 No.45186 again departs from Victoria with *THE SOUTH YORKSHIREMAN* on its somewhat leisurely late morning and early afternoon run to Marylebone in October 1958. The Stanier engine was a relative newcomer to the Leicester stud arriving there in June from Millhouses but in January 1959 it moved to Saltley and so was more liable to visit Sheffield again by way of the Midland route. The load of ten vehicles includes a Gresley kitchen car but the Up train was never very well patronised, because of its schedule and timings, unlike the Down train which left London quite late and was ideal for many business customers. *BLP 199.8.*

With the main line to Darnall running from left to right of the picture, fairly new EE Type 4 No.D208 comes off the SYR line from Rotherham at Woodburn junction on Saturday 11th October 1958. The 1-Co-Co-1 has charge of the 9.24 a.m. Hull-Sheffield (Victoria) passenger train which would change over to electric traction at Victoria and run on to Liverpool (Central) via Manchester (Central). This working was regularly used by Doncaster works, Monday to Friday, for testing the new diesels both during acceptance trials and after minor modifications when in normal service. By now though D208 was one of five EE Type 4 diesel-electrics used on *THE MASTER CUTLER* Pullman services during the week. However, the locomotive which brought the Friday evening 'Cutler' in from King's Cross (due Victoria 10.5 p.m.) was used intensively from 4.20 a.m. on Saturday morning until early Monday. The weekend fill-in turns started with an early Sheffield—Doncaster train followed by a 6.0 a.m. Doncaster—Hull service, returning to Victoria on the train shown here. Next would be an afternoon run to Leicester and back followed by the 6.10 p.m. goods to York. Another goods train, 8.30 p.m. York—Doncaster, positioned the diesel for the 12.54 a.m. Sunday morning Doncaster—King's Cross. Then the 1.20 p.m. KX—Grantham, 5.28 p.m. Grantham—KX, 11.55 p.m. KX—Doncaster from where, on arrival it made its way light to Sheffield early Monday morning to be in position to work the 7.20 a.m. Up 'Cutler' service to London. On delivery to British Railways from Vulcan Foundry to Doncaster, these big locomotives took the Rotherham route having come from Newton-le-Willows via the former LNWR main line from Earlstown to Manchester (Exchange)/(Victoria), Miles Platting, Ashburys, Guide Bridge, Woodhead and Sheffield (Victoria). Note the fly-over to Darnall motive power depot in the right background *BLP 203.1.*

It is early October 1958 and the newly dieselised and accelerated *MASTER CUTLER* Pullman service to King's Cross (7.20 a.m. ex Victoria) is a success but once the 'Cutler had arrived in London its stock and the locomotive hauling it were pressed back into service for a late morning service back to Sheffield (11.20 a.m. ex KX). Upon arrival in Sheffield the stock was serviced ready for the 3.20 p.m. departure back to King's Cross where the stock was made ready for the late evening 7.20 p.m. departure from KX back to Sheffield. The locomotive was taken off at KX and replaced by another, and was then put onto a new Diagram which involved a trip to Newcastle as the first job. To say that the new diagrams were intensive was, for the time, an understatement and as mentioned in the previous caption five locomotives were involved, each travelling just under 4,700 miles each week, something which steam locomotives were incapable of. This is D209 taking on water near Nunnery junction during its afternoon 'rest' prior to working the 3.20 p.m. Pullman to King's Cross. *BLP 205.8.*

On Wednesday 18th June 1958 British Railways Eastern Region staged an exhibition of motive power and rolling stock at Blast Lane goods depot. The star of the show (as far as BR was concerned) was English Electric 2,000 h.p. Type 4 No.D201, a recent addition to the ER fleet having arrived from the makers during the previous April. Immediately behind the 'Whistler' was a two-car diesel multiple unit, E51258/E56416, a new product from the nearby Cravens factory. Under cover and just inside the shed were a pair of Pullman cars, 1st Class *Rosamund* and 2nd Class No.303 - both from the *MASTER CUTLER* formation - took position behind the d.m.u. Over to the right can be seen brand new, Swindon built, and now Doncaster based double-chimneyed 9F No.92192. The 2-10-0 was to have a short life of just seven years but in this tenth year of BR's existence it was the latest of the steam motive power and still had a job to do. Hidden behind and on the track to the right of the Type 4 was EM1 Bo-Bo electric locomotive No.26026 which was ex Gorton works and wearing newly applied green livery. Representing the rapidly growing diesel shunter family was five-year old 350 h.p. 0-6-0DE No.D3063 which had only just been renumbered but was ex works with a fresh coat of green paint. The lack of public participation in the picture apparently stems from the fact that Keith Pirt took this picture on the day before the exhibition was open to the public, just as the setting up was completed (note the ceremonial bunting). *BLP 184.7.*

A close-up of D201, the bucket suggests that last minute cleaning is taking place but the big diesel is already immaculate with not only the body sides having reflective surfaces but the bogies too have a high sheen to them. As a public relations exercise BR must have found these exhibitions useful because they staged many more up and down the country. Enthusiasts, especially the younger elements (including this writer) found them very useful for getting onto BR premises to peruse the motive power without having to look over shoulders with an eye out for irate shed foremen. Initially allocated to Stratford depot for Great Eastern line workings to Norwich, D201 moved to Hornsey in May 1958 for ECML use. Its inclusion to the Sheffield exhibition was no coincidence as it was soon to take part in the dieselisation and rerouting of the accelerated *MASTER CUTLER* Pullman service. *BLP 184.6.*

Resplendent in shiny gloss black - the new way forward for steam was to keep it simple. Ten years after No.92192 had its image caught on film steam on British Railways was finished but back in 1958 the public was still encouraged to marvel at the achievements created by the nationalised railway industry. Admitted, the 2-10-0 did look 'the business' with even the bufferheads polished and its certain demise, in seven years hence, was far from everyone's mind - unthinkable even. Note the express freight headlamps which was a nice and appropriate touch. but, look at the position of the coupling rod - did no one realise that railway enthusiasts, especially the photographic fraternity, like to see coupling rods at the bottom of their arc! I wonder if the 9F had even had a fire lit yet? Note the new insulated fish van behind the tender, another fitting touch for both the headcode and what this locomotive would be hauling once operational. Remember the Kitmaster model of the 9F and the Hornby-Dublo insulated fish van? That was nearly fifty years ago! *BLP 184.5.*

Before the 'Brits' took over this daily working, B17 No.61643 CHAMPION LODGE brings the Harwich—Liverpool boat train into Sheffield (Victoria) and is passing No.5 signal box in early 1958. The March based 'Sandringham' was by now into its last months of operational life and would be condemned at Doncaster works during the coming summer.

After ten years of virtually monopolising the haulage of the Harwich (Parkeston Quay)—Liverpool (Central) boat train *THE NORTH COUNTRY CONTINENTAL* and its late afternoon return working, the March based Gresley B17s gave up the job to Eastern Region 'Britannia' Pacifics in the summer of 1958. By August the 'Brits' were appearing everyday and in this early September view of the Down service approaching Victoria, No.70009 ALFRED THE GREAT has charge of the boat train. Although based at both Norwich and Stratford, the GE Line 'Britannias' worked to Stratford Diagram No.6 for this train and started the job from Goodmayes yard departing at 2.55 a.m. with a 5.02 a.m. arrival at Parkeston. After servicing the Pacific departed Parkeston Quay with the 8.0 a.m. Down boat train service, arriving Sheffield (Victoria) 12.52 p.m. Detaching and handing over to electric traction (EM2 Co-Co), the 7P visited Darnall for servicing ready to take the Up train away from Victoria at the 3.30 p.m. departure time. Arrival in Harwich was at 8.53 p.m. with time then for further servicing before departing Parkeston at 11.40 p.m. Arrival in London (Spitalfields) was at 2.34 a.m. - twenty-one minutes short of 24 hours - but now requiring a fire clean which would preclude its participation on the same Diagram immediately. Hence there was never the same Britannia on the boat train two days running - magic. By Christmas 1958 all of the ER 'Brits' had visited Sheffield on this working. *BLP 197.1.*

Autumnal early morning mist (and industrial pollution) envelope the carriage sidings and the surrounding area east of Nunnery junction on Saturday 25th October 1958. The wet rails disappearing into the distance add to the picture where nothing is really identifiable including the BR Standard '5' getting ready to haul a rake of LMS coaches down to Midland station for a southbound service. Behind KRP the Victoria carriage pilot is propelling vehicles east from the station and it is a time to be careful for all concerned. *BLP 204.7.*

Later that morning we have a last look at the Pullman stock of *THE MASTER CUTLER*. The six vehicles in the fixed formation were: Brake 2nd No.70, Kitchen 2nd No.303, Kitchen 1st *Rosamund*, Kitchen 1st *Sappho*, Kitchen 1st *Plato*, Brake 2nd No.68. Surely if time machines were invented, would you not like to take a journey in one of those Pullman cars, being served breakfast and noting all that motive power outside the window? Having been stored at Victoria station overnight - it was well after 10.0 p.m. by the time the staff had vacated the cars - one of the first jobs on the Saturday morning was to take the formation for washing and J11 No.64329 is about to perform that duty propelling the train out of the station first. At 40 tons apiece, the six Pullman cars made a tidy load but that was well within the capabilities of the EE Type 4 and the other motive power which took over the Pullman workings after 1960, the uprated Brush Type 2s. *BLP 205.7.*

The Nunnery Colliery landsales yard in October 1958. Situated nearly a mile away from the pit head and right on the edge of Sheffield city centre, the yard was also alongside Blast Lane goods depot, seen on the right. The colliery itself had closed in 1953 after 113 years of production but landsales were continued with rail access via the Nunnery Colliery Railway. The bridges carrying this single track railway over the Midland main line and Nunnery curve can be seen elsewhere in this album but this was the ultimate destination of the railway. Note the period built Bedford flat bed household delivery trucks and the Commer tipping lorries parked up and all in the blue livery of the National Coal Board. The shunter goes about his work and is waiting for the 0-6-0T No.8 to pull a single wagon off the near siding for repositioning. The scene is certainly out of the past and no doubt in its day would have been ignored by 'spotters' because (a) it was industrial and (b) two main lines ran within a stones throw and BR locomotives were more plentiful, accessible and perhaps more interesting. Nowadays such a setting would draw enthusiasts from hundreds of miles distant and thousands of images would record every movement of the engine besides its surrounding environment. Luckily for us Keith Pirt took a great interest in his local railway scene and recorded much of what was happening including this - dare I say it - ideal model railway subject. *BLP 202.5.*

No.8 in close-up (yes the number is on the tank side somewhere, midway between cab entrance and the front of the tank) on the same date as the previous illustration. Looking less than its best, the outside cylinder 0-6-0T appeared extremely shabby. From photographic evidence its last overhaul and repaint took place back in 1955 or thereabouts. Three years on and the chances of another overhaul were not, apparently, in the offing. This locomotive had a somewhat interesting existence from new in 1911 when Hawthorn Leslie, their No.2879, was delivered to the Shropshire & Montgomery Light Railway. Numbered 6 by the Colonel Stephens' outfit, the 0-6-2T as she was then, was also named THISBE. Five years later the Government required the engines presence at Longmoor for military service during WWI. After the conflict the tank was purchased by the Mersey Docks & Harbour Board who in 1927 sold it to the Nunnery Colliery. At what stage of its life the 0-6-2T became an 0-6-0T is uncertain but the old lady worked alongside other second-hand 0-6-0 tank engines at the colliery and the landsales yard here. Inevitably old age and redundancy caught up with the Nunnery NCB locomotives and in April 1962 they were cut up on site by a local scrap merchant. *BLP 202.7.*

No.67439 back in October 1953 when fully lined but with what appears to be a rather severe scoring along the tank side. In fact this was a demarcation line indicating where a new piece of plating had been welded onto the bottom half of the tank in an effort to prevent leakage in what, by now, were nearly fifty years old water containers. The plate was added too (note the small patch towards the front of the tank) during a General overhaul in July 1952 and worked out to be a much cheaper solution to leakage than fabricating completely new tanks; the inside wall next to the boiler also had to dealt with too but at a 'General' this was easily accessible with the boiler absent for a couple of days at least. Most of the class suffered from the leakage problem and illustrations of other C13s will show how prevalent the problem was throughout the LNER and BR periods. *BLP 123.*

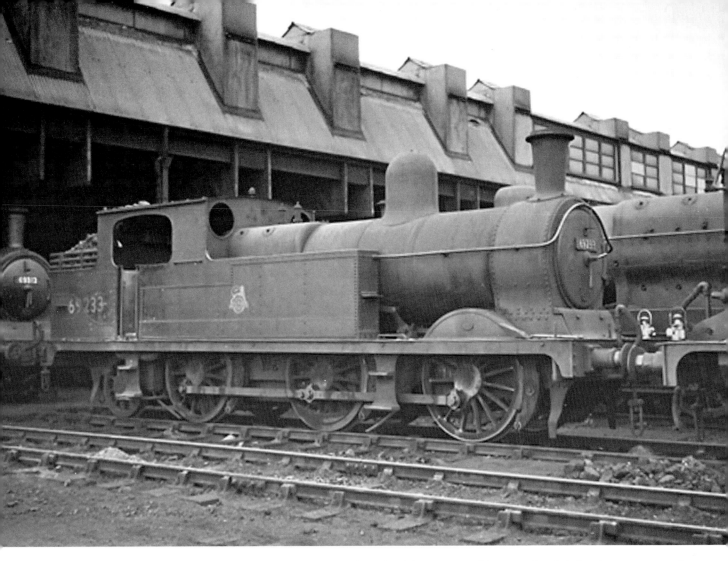

By the summer of 1958 most of Darnall's N5 fleet was either stored serviceable or were waiting to make their last journey across the Pennines to Gorton and oblivion. For instance Nos.69259, 69266, 69286, and 69361 were stored at the back of the shed and appeared ready for the final call whilst as many again were laid up at Staveley shed where ample room was available for storing Darnall's apparent outcasts but the withdrawals did not come to all of them during 1958 and a couple worked into the following year albeit erratically. Back in the summer of 1954 the last seven engines comprising N4 class faced oblivion also and all would be gone by the end of the year. N4 No.69233 is showing signs of its age outside the west end of the shed in the summer of 1954 but would last out until December. Besides working the local colliery trips around south Yorkshire, these engines also performed much of the shunting work in the area but the growing fleet of 0-6-0 diesel shunters allowed BR to condemn these 0-6-2 tanks along with the younger N5 class. But it must be said that this particular engine had given its worth because when this picture was captured on film it was already sixty-four years old. After making the journey over Woodhead to Gorton, where the infamous white crosses were painted on, No.69233 was then sent back to Yorkshire but to Doncaster works where it was cut up. *BLP 26H.8.3.*

On Sunday 4th September 1955 Tuxford based O4/7 No.63758 rests at the east end of Darnall shed. The 2-8-0 was on its way home after completing a month long General overhaul at Gorton. Allocated to Tuxford since January 1955, the O4/7 was one of the 1944 wartime conversions fitted with a Gresley 15D boiler in exchange for its original Robinson designed boiler. Purchased by the LNER in 1924, and numbered 6276, this engine had been built by the North British Locomotive Co. in December 1917 for the Ministry of Munitions. Its first LNER classification was O4 Part 3 simply because of its MofM origin, however, it was, for all intent and purpose, a GCR Class 8K heavy freight locomotive. Considering its rebuilding to Part 7, No.63758 was one of the early casualties of the class and was condemned in May 1962 just one day after arriving at Gorton works for repair. Its residency of Tuxford ended in February 1959 when that shed was closed. It then went to Langwith Junction but less than fifteen months later moved on to Immingham, its final depot. Except for four years spent at Doncaster shed from February 1946, the former ROD 2-8-0 had spent its LNER and BR years working from ex Great Central sheds. It was cut up at Gorton in June 1962. *BLP 98F.6.*

The 'dump' at Darnall shed was sometimes a place of much activity, although this illustration contradicts that statement. Situated at the west end of the depot, alongside the vehicular access road, the title 'dump' was appropriate in two ways [1] the amount of coal dumped from the locomotive tenders was literally 'dumped' (was it ever used again by BR?) [2] look at the number of 'dead' locomotives standing out in all weathers just rusting away. During the winter period especially, the activity here did step up a couple of notches and engines would be shunted onto the sidings after being capped off and tallowed down. Coal was shovelled from the tenders and then when a couple or more engines were laid up, they would be towed away to Staveley shed for winter storage either under cover or not depending on room. This is the dump in 1958 with a couple of 'Directors' Nos.62666 ZEEBRUGGE and 62667 SOMME, nearest the camera. Both are complete with name, number and shed plates. They have been made ready for winter storage and left uncleaned - the proven theory that grime and dirt does retard the rusting process, being employed - glass has been removed from side windows and coupling rods are still attached. No doubt the shed cleaners were used to empty the tenders hence the lack of clean locomotives at 41A. Further along the siding are a couple of K2s whilst in the other siding a 'Director' heads a line consisting a J39, another two D11 and a couple of K2. *BLP 165.8.*

Travelling to the extreme eastern outskirts of the city, near Beighton, we are looking south along the GCR main line towards Killamarsh North and South junctions. This was the start of the Manchester, Sheffield & Lincolnshire 'Derbyshire Lines' and its eventual thrust towards London. It is early evening in the latter days of August 1954 and Stanier Class 5 No.44694 is drifting downhill towards Beighton in charge of the Bournemouth—York which the 4-6-0 has brought from Leicester. Being a Low Moor engine, No.44694 would have brought the Up Bradford portion of *THE SOUTH YORKSHIREMAN* into Sheffield (Victoria) during the morning whereupon the Sheffield carriages, including kitchen and dining cars, were coupled to the Bradford portion and the new formation would them go forward to Marylebone with either a B1, A3 or even a V2 as motive power. After taking water at Victoria the Class 5 would them take the southbound York—Bournemouth to Leicester where Western Region motive power would take over. After servicing it would then work back northwards with this balancing turn in order to be at Victoria to haul the Bradford portion of the Down *TSY* back home. The rear vehicles of this train are just crossing the girder bridge spanning the original North Midland railway, out of sight just below the embankment east of the train. Across the open expanse of land to the left can be seen another line which was the GCR (LD&ECR) route linking Langwith Junction with Beighton. Until the end of WW2 there used to be a junction here, situated about where the locomotive is positioned, which took a GC branch off to the right and southwards to the now closed (1944) Holbrook Colliery. *BLP 20F.8.6.*

An unidentified Stanier Class 5 speeds through Canklow with an Up fitted freight in July 1956. We are now in the valley of the river Rather standing alongside the 'Old Road' of the North Midland Railway which by-passed Sheffield by about eight miles. In the background is Rotherham Main Colliery. This is one of the earliest stretches of main line railway in Britain and even now it carries much of the country's rail freight traffic being a major north-south artery. One of BR's first dabbles with door-to-door containerisation in the shape of the erstwhile *CONDOR* ran these rails during the hours of darkness - at least the Down train did, the Up train ran through Midland station - in the early days of dieselisation. Now long gone, along with the somewhat unreliable Metrovick Co-Bo diesels which hauled the week nights-only service, the train was a success of sorts in that it proved that the concept worked. Apparently it even made a profit for BR! *BLP 121F.13.*

43

There were plenty of coking plants in this area of Yorkshire during the early 1950s and Toton based 4F No.44200 heads for home with a loaded train of coke in high capacity hoppers in July 1956. The commissioning of the Avenue coking plant (Coal Preparation Plant to give it the NCB title) near Chesterfield did not take place until the late 1950s so much of the industry around the East Midlands and North Derbyshire had to rely on the output of the plants attached to the coal mines in Yorkshire and North Derbyshire. Rotherham Main had its own coking plant with twenty-eight ovens (note the chimney belching out some of the waste from the process) able to produce 150,000 tons of coke per annum but that was small beer compared with many of the other local plants, some of which had two and three times that capacity. Besides the all important coke being produced, more than twenty other by-products, including gases and liquids, would be manufactured during the process. Remember that coking plant aroma. *BLP 121F.12.*

During the late afternoon a Down mixed freight with Canklow 4F No.44013 heads towards Masboro sidings and is crossing over Canklow junction which contained Canklow Goods Lines junction and Engine Shed junction. The track nearest the camera is the Down goods with a set of points facilitating the entrance to Canklow engine shed and forming the latter named junction. This was essentially the start of a heavily industrialised stretch of railway with yards, junctions and numerous sidings stretching over a number of miles. Although the 4F is 'pegged' for the main line, it may have been proceeding to the sidings via the turn-out at Masboro Sorting signal box. *BLP 121F.10.*

The North Midland Railway by-passed Sheffield at first but eventually entered the city from the Chesterfield direction as well as from the north and east. However the early main line through Rotherham continued to be the main artery for through freight traffic. Canklow engine shed was created to cater for the growing mineral and exchange traffic using nearby Masboro sidings and since May 1840 there had been a locomotive servicing facility in the area. The first known shed building was built around 1855 near what became Masbrough South junction to house one engine but this establishment was replaced by a two road shed in 1881. By the time larger premises were required, the Midland Railway had to build on a piece of land some distance to the south of Masbrough and that establishment opened in 1900. Known as Canklow, the shed was a typical MR square roundhouse of the latest design, with three pitched roof bays covering a 50ft diameter turntable from which radiated twenty-four stabling roads. A single sided coaling stage was provided in the usual MR fashion with a wagon ramp and covered accommodation for the coalmen. The stage sufficed until closure of the depot in 1965, no mechanical apparatus ever being installed. Though daily visitors from Hasland and Toton, the LMS Garratts had to make do with stabling in the shed yard, their length precluding them from the covered accommodation in any of the roundhouses except Toton. In this Sunday, 29th May 1955 view, Hasland's No.47986 rests on the road parallel with the coaling road on the east side of the site, north of the shed. *BLP 52F.8.6.*

On the west side of the coaling stage, at a slightly lower level, two other sidings were provided for engines not able to be accommodated in the roundhouse. Built for the 0-6-0 tender engine for which there was adequate room in Midland days, the depot's allocation grew to more than twice what its covered accommodation could offer so that during ant weekend as many as sixty plus locomotives were resident with less than half under cover. This is long-time resident No.43814 sharing one of the stabling roads with a couple of 4Fs, an 8F and others. Besides more than thirty 0-6-0 tender engines being allocated, there was also a handful of 0-6-0T of both Midland and LMS origins. The Stanier 8Fs were the latest additions which during the last five years of the depot's existence, were joined by WD Austerity 2-8-0s which replaced many of the ageing 3F 0-6-0s. Before the Stanier 8F arrived to take over most of the long distance hauls, Canklow had five of the Fowler 7F 0-8-0s, the so-called 'Austin Sevens'. A one time the depot was also home to one of the former LNWR G2 0-8-0s. *BLP 52F.8.7.*   47

Half-cab 1F No.41835 visits its home shed, Canklow, for some refreshment in 1956. The roundhouse stands out of frame to the left, whilst the shed offices form the background for the engine. Note the British Railways road vehicle which could be either a bus or van. The ramp for vehicular access to the public road goes off to the right. Canklow roundhouse stood derelict for many years after steam and indeed BR had vacated the place. Up to the late 70's its walls stood forlorn whilst the roof cladding slowly decayed, however, it did give the interested observer a chance to see the layout of the roof trussing employed in this final version of Midland Railway roundhouse. *BLP 122F.2.*

The rear of Canklow roundhouse in with an assortment of local engines stabling, or in some cases stored, on the single road which projected from the rear of the shed. The line-up is headed by Johnson Class 2 No.58238, one of the 4ft 11in. diameter wheel types dating from the mid-1880s; note that the tender is virtually empty of coal. All the other engines, though unidentified numerically, are also former MR 0-6-0s of varying vintages. Such was the lot of this depot until LMS days when larger engines appeared. Prior to that double-heading had been the norm for many MR goods trains. No.58238 had done its work for three masters and its days were nearly at an end. Withdrawal took place in November 1957. Note that when the shed was built that enough land was cut away to allow another roundhouse to be built on this side. *BLP 125F.3.*

Ivatt 2MT No.41274 at bay platform 3 at Midland station in early 1958 with a working to Barnsley (Court House). Having shared the service with the Barnsley based C14 tanks, the Class 2MT worked this route until diesel multiple units eventually ousted them. With snow still clinging on to the canopies the apparent cold is highlighted by the escaping steam silhouetting the 2-6-2T, the cab of which would have been a nice place to be on that day. Royston supplied the motive power for these workings and push-pull fitted No.41274 went new to that depot in September 1950. Although initially joined by No.41273, that engine left Royston in May 1954 for Skipton but Nos.41281 and 41282 took its place in November 1955 after a year at Lees working the 'Delph Donkey'. All three Ivatt tanks left Royston in June 1959 when the diesel multiple units took over their work. Note the absence of the overall roof over platforms 1 and 2 over on the right. This, of course, was the new (1904) section of the enlarged station which was not afforded the same cover as the original 1870 part of the station. *BLP 168.3.*

It would be interesting to know the story behind this event at Midland station on 4th September 1954 when Haymarket based Peppercorn A1 No.60162 SAINT JOHNSTOUN, ex Doncaster works after General overhaul (26th July to 27th August), visited the city. Seen passing the North Junction signal box, the Pacific was photographed leaving the station for the north with a train of varied passenger stock. It appears to be double-headed by a Thompson B1 but the LNER Group Standard tender could also have belonged to a Peppercorn K1, J39 or even an O2, although the latter was quite unlikely. Note that the second vehicle appears to be wearing roofboards. The signal box was apparently the fourth such structure on the site and dated from 1912, its predecessors dated from the opening of the station in 1870, an enlarged box appeared in 1893 followed by another in 1904 when station enlargement was taking place, the latter boxes seem to have had fairly short operational lives even allowing for expansion of the station. Although the southern approaches to Midland station were expanded, the restrictions at the north end remain to this day with little change during the past one hundred and thirty-odd years. *BLP 21F.8.3.*

Bristol Barrow Road 'Jubilee' No.45651 SHOVELL arrives on platform 6 at Midland station from Leeds with a West of England service in 1956. Water is being replenished in the tender during the five minute station stop. Note the proximity of the housing looming above the retaining wall. Part of the curved overall roof spanning the east side of the station, but not platform 9, can be seen to the left. Already sections are being removed to open up the station into the establishment we know today. The public footbridge above the first coach linked Granville Street with Turner Street. This vantage point would have been ideal for photographers but seems to have been rarely used for such purposes. *BLP 113F.6.*

No.45651 had plenty of steam to spare as it departed from Midland station, crossing onto the Up fast line and headed for home with its afternoon express. The massive buttressed retaining walls, built during the creation of the station for its 1870 opening, are evidenced here by the scale of the stonework compared to the locomotive and its train. The later expansion of the station chose the less difficult direction - west towards the city centre. *BLP 113F.3.*

Using the Up slow, Royston based Stanier 2-6-2 Class 3 tank No.40181 takes a Chinley 'local' up the grade towards Millhouses in April 1958. We are about a mile south of Midland station, just north of Heeley the next intermediate station. The position of our photographer, Keith Pirt (yes, he did have lineside passes, loads of common sense but no conspicuity jacket), between the Up [on the right] and Down [left] fast lines, gives us a chance to see the descent of the Down fast before it threads beneath Charlotte Road bridge then briefly disappears underground, veering north and west under the Up and Down slow lines, finally to reappear as in the previous illustration on the west side of the railway. *BLP 169.8.*

Bursting out from beneath Charlotte Road bridge in April 1958, Saltley Class 5 No.44660 starts to work hard as it hauls *THE DEVONIAN* up the continuous 1 in 100 grade all the way to the southern portal of Bradway tunnel - five and a half miles away. To the left of the engine can be seen the railings which line the top of the cutting retaining wall of the Down fast diveunder. Since the end of steam on BR, the southern approaches to Midland station have undergone further change but in a negative direction with so-called 'rationalisation'. The quadruple lines from Dore & Totley to Midland station were doubled with loops set a couple of points along the route. The diveunder was no longer required and was taken out of use in June 1972. Still, it was useful while it lasted. Perhaps future traffic will see a requirement for more tracks on the approach to Midland but better signalling, faster and shorter trains (multiple units), and the lack of freight trains, which use other routes now, make the need for further trackwork seem a million miles away. *BLP 169.3*.

'Jubilee' No.45590 TRAVANCORE hurries off to Millhouses shed, some two miles distant, in April 1958 after bringing a train into Midland from the north. The condition of the engine leads one to believe that the 4-6-0 had recently undergone overhaul and repaint at main works. No.45590 had been a Millhouses engine since May 1947, except for a short couple of week-long transfers to Nottingham and Derby depots in February and March 1951. On the closure of 41C it moved across to Canklow in December 1961 but within three months had transferred across the Pennines to Lancashire where prospects for steam locomotives were still reasonable. Agecroft, Newton Heath and Warrington Dallam sheds used it over the next four years. *BLP 170.5.*

Before the coming of the diesels, the Stanier 'Jubilee' class was the mainstay of the express motive power on the Sheffield—London and the West of England express passenger trains. On a sunny April day in 1958, No.45682 TRAFALGAR of Barrow Road shed, heads for home with a West of England bound train in the early afternoon. Gathering pace along the Up fast, the 4-6-0 will not be home until the evening with calls to be made at Chesterfield, Derby, Burton-on-Trent, Birmingham, Cheltenham, Gloucester and finally Bristol (Temple Meads) - all the way running over former Midland Railway metals. By the time the 'Jubilee gets on shed at Barrow Road its tender will be virtually empty of coal whereas the water tank will have been replenished en route. All ten vehicles in the formation appear to be of LMS origin. Note that the passenger coaches in the headshunt appear to be of Great Western and Western Region origin. *BLP 170.3.*

With their crews seemingly not reading the road, these two engines reverse upgrade to Millhouses shed in April 1958. Both are LMS built but from different periods (just) and different designers. 4-4-0 No.40691 of Hasland shed was one of the final batch of 2P 4-4-0s which had its origins in the Johnson period of the MR. It was built at Crewe in 1932 when Derby still ran the LMS and was one of 138 such locomotives turned out between 1928 and 1932. The Millhouses 'Jubilee' No.45570 NEW ZEALAND was built just two years after the 2P by North British Locomotive Co. to the design of William Stanier who hauled LMS locomotive design into the 20th century. It would be interesting to know how these two ended up coupled together, making their combined way to shed. Most probably the 4-4-0 was attached at Chesterfield to help the possibly ailing 4-6-0 over the summit to Bradway tunnel. On the other hand the 4-4-0 may well have arrived at Midland station separately from No.45570 and the two were coupled together and released onto the main line to save line occupation - a regular occurrence at certain locations during busy periods. *BLP 170.2.*

Filthy 'Jubilee' No.45725 REPULSE (from where else but Millhouses) and another, rather cleaner, but unidentified member of the class work hard as they bite into the adverse gradient towards Heeley with a morning southbound express in April 1958. On either side of the railway here factories and building supplies yards contain the necessary materials which will soon help to modernise and change the skyline of Sheffield, for better or worse. *BLP 169.5.*

3F No.43745 collects a brakevan after working a goods train into the reception roads at Queens Road goods yard in April 1958. A dirty Grimesthorpe based DE 0-6-0 shunter No.13254 is the duty shunter, one of four Derby built 350 h.p. 0-6-0DE (13251—13254) which went new to Grimesthorpe shed in June 1956 when the Midland Lines, other than Toton, were having a share of the new and ever growing fleet of diesel motive power. The shunter was renumbered D3254 in September 1959 and worked around the Sheffield area for most of its career, ending up at Barrow Hill as 08186 and being withdrawn from there in March 1985 - just short of thirty years in service. The 3F was also a newcomer to Grimesthorpe allocation having arrived in the September of 1956 from Derby, however, it was not long for this world being withdrawn in October 1958. After rusting at Derby for nearly eight months, it was sold to a scrapyard in Scotland and hauled north in July 1959. Queens Road goods was situated on the west side of the line south of Midland station and opened in 1892 when the economy in the UK was booming. In 1958 the whole of the London Midland territory in Sheffield was handed over to Eastern Region control and plans were drawn up to rationalise the movement and distribution of freight in the newly formed Sheffield District. The plan envisaged one goods depot, one marshalling yard and one motive power depot by 1965. Closure of Queens Road took effect from 11th May 1965 even though the centralised goods depot planned for Grimesthorpe was still not built. Two more of the Sheffield area goods depots also closed during that year, Pond Street and Park Goods. Their closure reflected the gradual loss of goods traffic to road transport rather than the planned rationalisation of local services. *BLP 169.1.*

Saltley Stanier Class 5 No.44966 puts up a fine exhaust as it accelerates past Millhouses shed with a southbound express on a very cold day in January 1959. The sky is laden with what appears to be a lot of snow which, in this area of the country, could cause massive disruption and often did; the Hope valley line especially was susceptible to drifting snow. Millhouses shed would have to turnout two sometime three locomotives coupled together, with a plough at each end of the formation, and send them off to tackle the drifts. *BLP 207.2.*

A cold but unusually sunny 14th November 1954 found these three engines in winter storage in the south-west corner of Millhouses shed yard. It is another Sunday, the only day when many enthusiasts could get out to visit the sheds. Keith Pirt did not have far to travel in order to come across an engine shed and Millhouses was one such establishment where photographic freedom, courtesy of more than passing acknowledgement with the management, was useful. In the line-up here are LMS built compounds Nos.41063 and 41071, both wearing the compulsory chimney covering. Last in line is ex MR 2F No.58216 which appears to have a run-in with a paint brush. The latter engine was a fairly recent acquisition from Derby shed but it did not stay too long at 19B, transferring to Royston in June 1956. Both 4-4-0s came out of storage successfully No.41063 during the following February when it transferred to Manningham, whilst No.41071 helped out with the summer services at Sheffield until it too moved on, in April 1956, to Holbeck. Note the sludge carrier on the left of the picture, a necessary piece of equipment at Millhouses where a water softener was installed. It appears that the contents of the carrier have, for some years, been dumped by the track side. *BLP 28H.8.5.*

Just a bit further along the yard, and visible in the previous illustration, was Ivatt LMS 2MT No.41209. This 2-6-2T had arrived at Millhouses during the previous summer to join long standing residents Nos.41245 and 41246. The last of the initial and only LMS built batch, No.41209 was built in 1947 so could claim to be the last LMS built engine of its kind. However, sentiments regarding railway locomotives and equipment are something only enthusiasts could afford because these things had to earn their keep - something that most steam locomotives built after WW2 rarely did before being scrapped. This engine left Millhouses in December 1961 and eventually ended up in Western Region territory, albeit a section then under LMR control. Withdrawn in July 1965 it ended its days in a scrapyard in Swansea. *BLP 28H.8.6.*

'Jubilee' No.45609 GILBERT AND ELLIS ISLANDS is serviced and ready for another southbound working at Millhouses shed on Sunday morning, 13th February 1955. This engine shared, with No.45665, the distinction of having the longest name in the class, although the latter engine held the title for some time as it was named in 1935 whereas our subject was not named until the following year after running around nameless for a couple of years. No.45609 was one of those coupled, from new, to a 3500 gallon Fowler type tender (No.4566) with straight sides which, in this writer's opinion, somewhat spoilt the appearance of the locomotive - it seems the Derby spirit was never allowed to die on the LMS, even with the more modern Stanier designs. This locomotive had another distinction, as yet to be realised, and dubious to boot, in that it was the first of the class to be withdrawn in normal circumstances. No.45637 WINDWARD ISLANDS had of course succumb after the Harrow disaster in 1952 but G&EI was the only 'Jubilee' to be condemned in 1960. Transferring to Millhouses in September 1950 from Kentish Town, the 4-6-0 had spent the whole of its life from January 1935, working on the Midland Lines. Its usual tasks whilst on Millhouses books included the St Pancras expresses and the south-west bound trains such as *THE DEVONIAN* or *THE CORNISHMAN* as far south as Bristol in conjunction with the Barrow Road 'Jubilees'. *BLP 34H.8.8.*

Stabled a bit further down the yard on that same Sunday was exMR Johnson 0-4-4T No.58080. This example had a Belpaire boiler and although fairly dirty, the engine was nicely lined out. Discernible on the tank side is the lettering of the former owners LMS. This 0-4-4T had come to Millhouses in November 1953 from Burton-on-Trent and was soon to depart to Wellingborough where, just ten months from the date of this photograph, it was withdrawn. In days gone by the space from which KRP took this shot would have been covered in coal, stacked about eight to ten feet high, but disputes in the mining industry since Nationalisation along with shortages for other reasons, meant that the once tidy and large coal stacks held at each depot had to be used hence the untidy mess in the foreground. Behind the tank stands the bulk of the large double sided coaling stage built for the opening of the depot and never replaced by modern appliances. Note one of the depot's trio of Ivatt tanks, No.41246, sharing the rails with No.58080. *BLP 34H.8.6.*

On 18th December 1955, Grimesthorpe 2F No.58190 was visiting Millhouses shed and had obviously been refreshed at the coal stage. Goods engines were rarely allocated to Millhouses, the needs of the Goods Department on the former LMS lines in Sheffield being met by Grimesthorpe and Canklow depots. So the appearance of this engine was worth recording on film. The reason for its visit is unknown and the fact that it is stabled on the western side of the yard hints that it could have been collecting locomotives ready for workshops. The 0-6-0 moved to Barrow-in-Furness in May 1957 and within a couple of years became yet another withdrawal statistic. However, it came back to Sheffield in May 1960 when its new owner T.W.Ward (Scrap Merchant) brought the ancient engine to a yard in Killamarsh for cutting up. *BLP 109H.4.*

Nottingham based LMS Compound No.41185 rests at Millhouses shed in June 1956 in glorious morning sunshine. The 4-4-0 was about to transfer to Rowsley shed where its haulage of passenger trains would be somewhat limited, as indeed they were because just one year later it was reallocated to Derby where, after just four months, it was condemned during November 1957. Since its opening in 1901, Millhouses shed had a respectable number of Class 2 4-4-0s allocated but it was not until LMS days that the Class 4 compounds started to become residents. Numbers slowly built up so that just before the coming of the Stanier 'Jubilees' nearly a dozen were allocated. By 1956 the total had dwindled to four but visiting engines such as this helped the shed to keep its Midland flavour even though LMS and BR 'Standard' types were taking over. *BLP 125F.2*

Horwich built BR Standard Class 4 No.76088, of Trafford Park shed, was a regular visitor to Sheffield (Midland), working in from Manchester (Central) on the Hope Valley stopping passenger trains. New to Trafford Park in May 1957, along with Nos.76087 and 76089, the 2-6-0s worked these services until dieselisation ousted them in 1960. Seen here at Millhouses shed in March 1958, the Class 4 is in the usual Trafford Park livery of grime over black. In September 1962 the three Standards left Manchester and were sent south, two to Cricklewood and one (76087) to Woodford Halse, but the ever changing motive power situation on BR saw them having a number of homes before the inevitable withdrawals took place. Of the trio this engine lasted the longest and was condemned in June 1967, just ten years old. *BLP 171.8.*

Kentish Town Class 5 No.45447 passes over the catch points near Millhouses Park in early June 1955 as it gets a late morning St Pancras bound express underway. The Stanier 4-6-0 was no stranger to this route and was on loan to 14B for the summer only from Grimesthorpe shed. After three months working from Crewe North shed after delivery in December 1937, No.45447 transferred to Saltley for a fifteen year stint. In May 1953 Holbeck had its services until July 1954 when it moved to 19A. After its loan period to 14B it returned to Sheffield only to make a permanent move to Kentish Town in May 1956. Saltley got it back in November 1959, this time for nearly six years after which it left the Midland Lines and went to Holyhead in June 1965. This was followed by Shrewsbury in September 1966 and then Kingmoor in March 1967. Its big break came in January 1968 when it joined the elite at Rose Grove and became one of the last operational steam locomotives on British Railways. *BLP 53P.8.2.*

LMS Compound No.41073 wheels a Down semi-fast out of Bradway tunnel and round the curve at Dore & Totley during the late afternoon whilst Holbeck 'Jubilee' No.45597 BARBADOS speeds *THE THAMES-CLYDE EXPRESS* southwards in July 1956. To say that this area of Sheffield is rather nice would be an understatement. Although man has made his mark with the railway and some housing, the place appears to be tranquil (in between trains). *BLP 125F.8.*

Its the turn of the Down service of *THE DEVONIAN* now with immaculate Barrow Road 'Jubilee' No.45685 BARFLUER getting assistance from 4F No.44244. So much for tranquillity, this is the sixth passenger train in the last hour. Dore & Totley South Junction signal box nestles in the tree-lined cutting guarding the junction of the west curve onto the Hope Valley line. *BLP 125F.11.*

It is April 1956 and Toton based Garratt No.47982 traverses the 23-chain west curve from the Hope Valley line at Dore & Totley to gain the Up main line to Chesterfield with a train of empty mineral wagons from Gowhole sidings. The engine is about to enter the short Dore tunnel, the mouth of which is immediately behind our intrepid cameraman. Regular visitors to Gowhole with coal trains from the East Midlands pits, the Garratts were choosy about where they went. Gowhole was about as far north and west for their travels whereas York, via the old North Midland route, became their north-eastern boundary. Crewe works was their maintenance base and that was the limit of travel onto the former LNWR lines. The southern extreme was of course Cricklewood whilst in the south and west they were known to have got down to Gloucester, though rarely. Peterborough in the east was sometimes visited via Melton Mowbray. Note that the 'Garratts did not carry a shedplate on any part of their front panels. *BLP 146.6.*